# THE MYSTERIES OF THE

# *Universe*

# POSTER BOOK

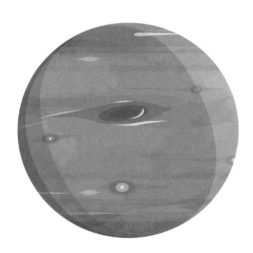

**Senior Acquisitions Editor** James Mitchem
**Editor** Becca Arlington
**Senior Designer** Ann Cannings
**US Senior Editor** Shannon Beatty
**Jacket Coordinator** Elin Woosnam
**Jacket Designer** Elle Ward
**Picture Research** Rituraj Singh, Sakshi Saluja
**Production Editor** Dragana Puvacic
**Senior Production Controller** Leanne Burke

First American Edition, 2024
Published in the United States by DK Publishing
1745 Broadway, 20th Floor, New York, NY 10019

Copyright © 2024 Dorling Kindersley Limited
DK, a Division of Penguin Random House LLC
24 25 26 27 10 9 8 7 6 5 4 3 2 1
001–343615–Sep/2024

Published in Great Britain by Dorling Kindersley Limited

Material used in this book was previously published in:
*The Mysteries of the Universe* (2020)

A catalog record for this book
is available from the Library of Congress.
ISBN: 978-0-5938-4954-5

Printed and bound in China

www.dk.com

DK would like to thank the following for their contributions to the original *Mysteries of the Universe*: Will Gater for the text; Daniel Long and Angela Rizza for the illustrations.

The publisher would like to thank the following for their kind permission to reproduce their photographs:
(Key: a-above; b-below/bottom; c-center; f-far; l-left; r-right; t-top)

3 ESO: Y. Beletsky. 5 Science Photo Library: Walter Pacholka, Astropics. 7 NASA. 9 NASA: SDO / AIA / S. Wiessinger. 11 ESO: P. Horálek / Solar Wind Sherpas project. 13 NASA: Goddard Space Flight Center. 15 NASA: JPL. 17 NASA: JPL-Caltech. 19 NASA: JPL-Caltech / MSSS. 21 NASA: JPL-Caltech / SwRI / MSSS / Gerald Eichstadt / Sean Doran © CC NC NA. 23 NASA: JPL-Caltech / Space Science Institute. 25 NASA: JPL / Space Science Institute. 27 NASA: JPL (tr); JPL-Caltech (bl). 29 NASA: Johns Hopkins University Applied Physics Laboratory / Southwest Research Institute. 31 NASA: JPL-Caltech / ESA / CXC / STScI. 33 NASA: ESA and A. Nota (STScI / ESA). 35 NASA and The Hubble Heritage Team (AURA/STScI): NASA, ESA and AURA / Caltech. 37 ESO: L. Calçada. 39 NASA: ESA, N. Smith (University of Arizona) and J. Morse (BoldlyGo Institute). 41 Science Photo Library: EHT Collaboration / European Southern Observatory. 43 ESO. 45 NOIRLab: T.A.Rector (NOIRLab / NSF / AURA) and Hubble Heritage Team (STScI / AURA / NASA). 47 ESO: Igor Chekalin. 49 NASA: JPL-Caltech / S. Stolovy (Spitzer Science Center / Caltech). 51 NASA and The Hubble Heritage Team (AURA/STScI): NASA, ESA, and the Hubble Heritage Team (STScI / AURA). 53 Ken Crawford. 55 Robert Gendler. 57 NASA and The Hubble Heritage Team (AURA/STScI): NASA, ESA, and the Hubble Heritage (STScI / AURA)-ESA / Hubble Collaboration. 59 NASA and The Hubble Heritage Team (AURA/STScI): NASA, ESA, and The Hubble Heritage Team (STScI / AURA); Acknowledgment: W. Keel (University of Alabama, Tuscaloosa). 61 NASA: ESA, and the Hubble SM4 ERO Team. 63 NASA and The Hubble Heritage Team (AURA/STScI): NASA, ESA, and J. Lotz and the HFF Team (STScI)

Cover images: *Front:* Ken Crawford; bl: Fotolia: eevl tl: NASA and The Hubble Heritage Team (AURA/STScI): NASA, ESA and AURA / Caltech bc, NASA, ESA, and the Hubble Heritage Team (STScI / AURA) br, NASA, ESA, J. DePasquale (STScI), and R. Hurt (Caltech / IPAC) tc; NASA: Johns Hopkins University Applied Physics Laboratory / Carnegie Institution of Washington tr, JPL-Caltech / ESA, the Hubble Heritage Team (STScI / AURA) cra, STScI / AURA cla; Science Photo Library: Walter Pacholka, Astropics cr; *Back:* Science Photo Library: Walter Pacholka, Astropics cr

All other images © Dorling Kindersley Limited

## Poster list

 The night sky

 Meteors

 Auroras

 The Sun

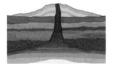 Total solar eclipse

 The transit of Mercury

 Volcanoes on Venus

 Valles Marineris

 Exploring Mars

 Swirling clouds

 Saturn

 Iapetus

 Neptune and Uranus

 Pluto

 The Milky Way

 Stars

 Star clusters

 Birth of a planet

 Eta Carinae

 Black hole

 Globular cluster

 Dark nebula

 Reflection nebula

 Galactic Center

 The Pillars of Creation

 Supernova remnant

 The Andromeda Galaxy

 Spiral galaxy

 Lenticular galaxy

 Stephan's Quintet

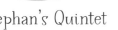 Gravitational lens

# The night sky

Humans first turned telescopes toward the night sky around 400 years ago. The dazzling view on the other side of this poster is from the Atacama Desert in Chile.

# Meteors

Meteor showers occur when Earth passes through a trail of dust left behind by a comet or asteroid. Pictured on the reverse of this poster is a bright meteor falling during the Geminid meteor shower, which occurs every December.

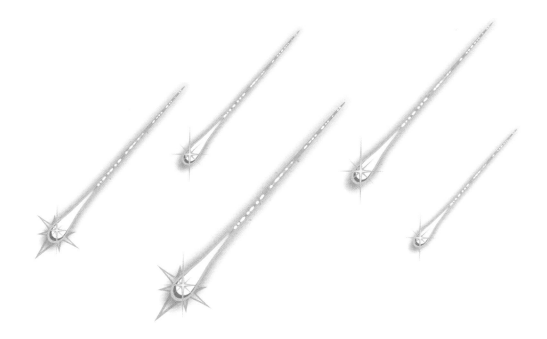

# Auroras

The green color of auroras, which are softly glowing curtains of light, comes from glowing oxygen gas. The reverse of this poster shows a view of the aurora borealis, taken from the International Space Station.

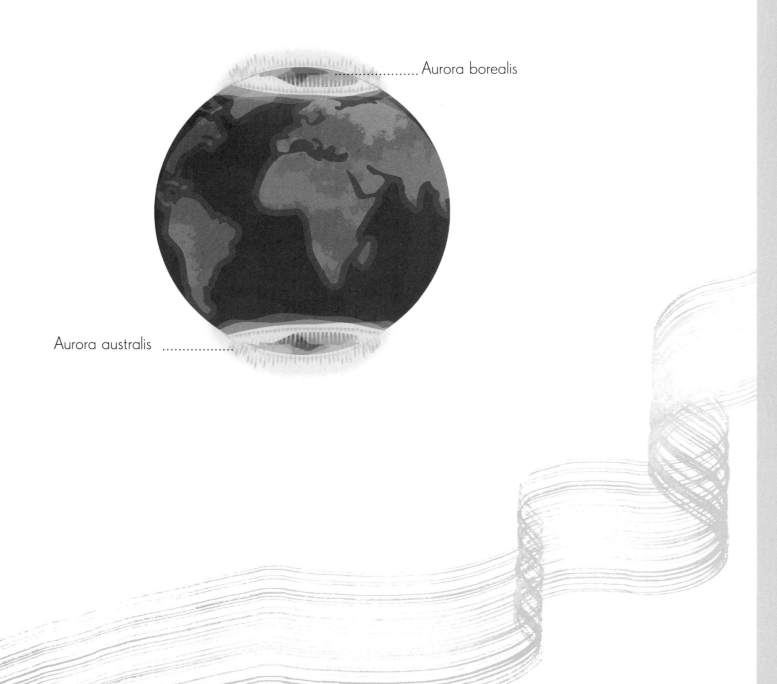

............... Aurora borealis

Aurora australis ..................

# The sun

Astronomers think that our galaxy's star, the sun,
will live for about another 5 billion years. The image on
the other side of this poster was made by combining 25
photographs to show a year of activity on the sun.

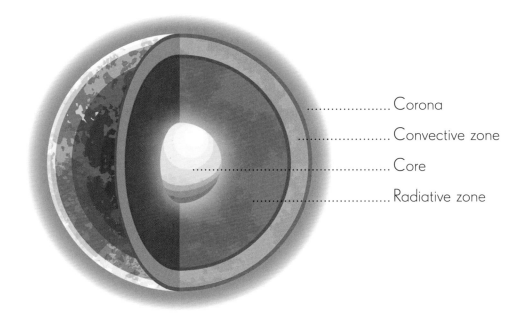

.................... Corona

.................... Convective zone

.................... Core

.................... Radiative zone

# Total solar eclipse

The white wisps around the moon during a total solar eclipse are part of the sun's outer atmosphere, known as the corona. Pictured on the other side of this poster is a total solar eclipse from 2016, seen from Indonesia.

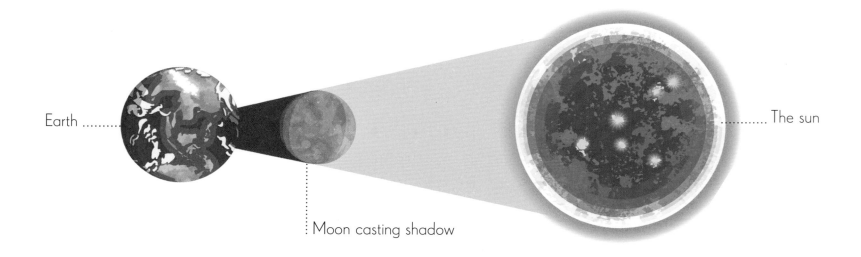

Earth

Moon casting shadow

The sun

# The transit
# of Mercury

As Mercury and Venus whirl around the sun, they sometimes
swoop in front of its face from the perspective of Earth.
These transits are quite rare, and the last one, shown
on the reverse of this poster, was in 2019.

Mercury is the fastest planet as it moves
around the sun, so it was named after
the Roman messenger god, Mercury.

# Volcanoes on Venus

Most of planet Venus is covered in solidified lava, and there are many ancient volcanoes. One of the tallest is called Maat Mons, after the Egyptian goddess of truth, Ma'at.

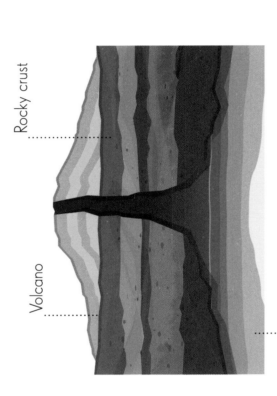

Rocky crust

Volcano

Magma chamber

# Valles Marineris

Valles Marineris is an immense, deep canyon that stretches an astonishing 1,367 miles (2,200 km) across Mars. It is larger than the entire length of Italy. It looks like a huge scar on the planet's surface.

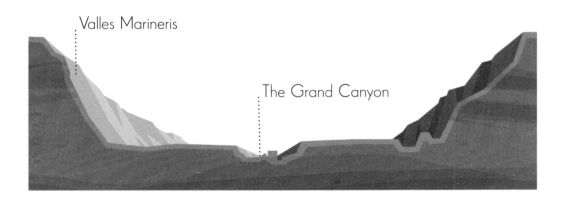

Valles Marineris

The Grand Canyon

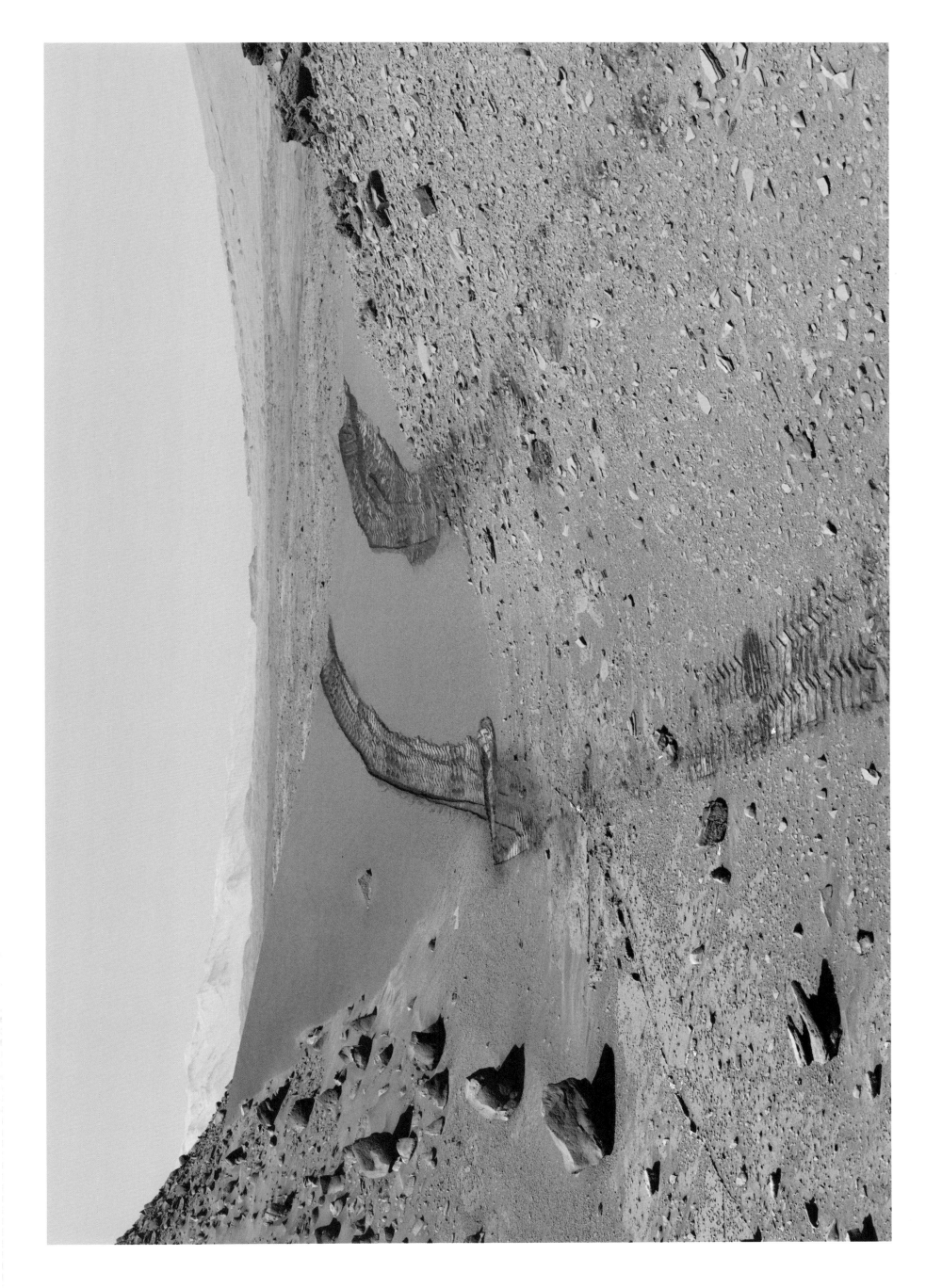

# Exploring Mars

NASA's Curiosity rover landed on Mars in 2012 to find out about conditions on the planet. Mars's color comes from iron oxide in its soil—this is what makes rust orangey-red.

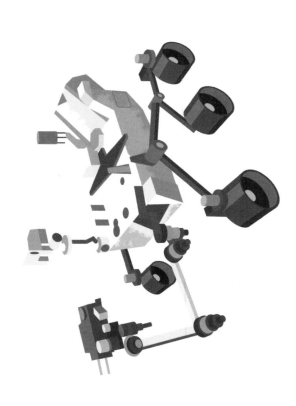

# Swirling clouds

Jupiter's atmosphere is mostly made up of hydrogen and helium. Huge swirls and pastel-colored ripples can be seen from above the planet, and the other side of this poster shows the clouds of Jupiter in its northern hemisphere.

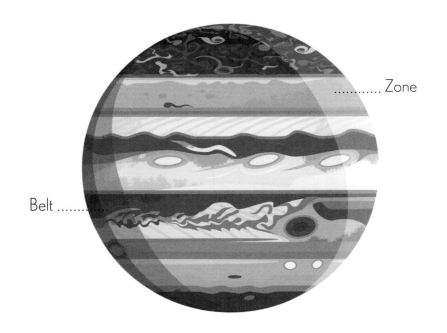

............. Zone

Belt .............

# Saturn

Encircled by an exquisite system of rings, Saturn is the second largest planet in our solar system. The unusual photo of Saturn on the other side of this poster was taken while the sun was behind the planet.

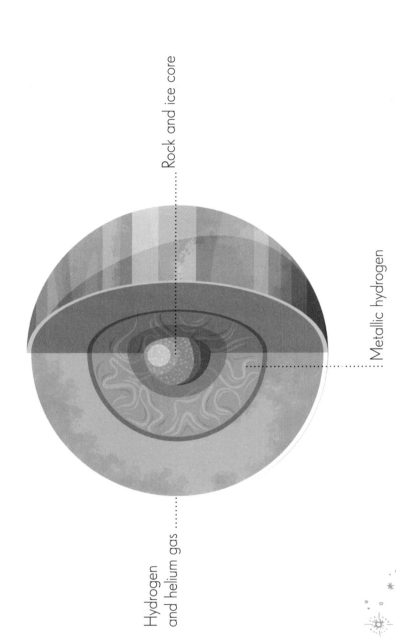

Rock and ice core

Metallic hydrogen

Hydrogen and helium gas

# Iapetus

Saturn's moon, Iapetus, travels around Saturn at a distance of over 2.2 million miles (3.5 million km)—that's more than nine times the distance between the Earth and the moon.

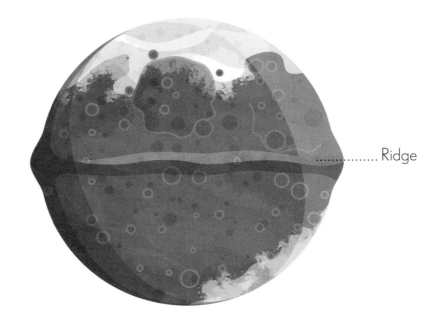

............... Ridge

# Neptune and Uranus

It's difficult to imagine how far away from the sun Neptune is—around 2.8 billion miles (4.5 billion km). Next in line, and almost half as far, is Uranus. Uranus has the largest axial tilt in the solar system, which may mean it was once smashed into by another world.

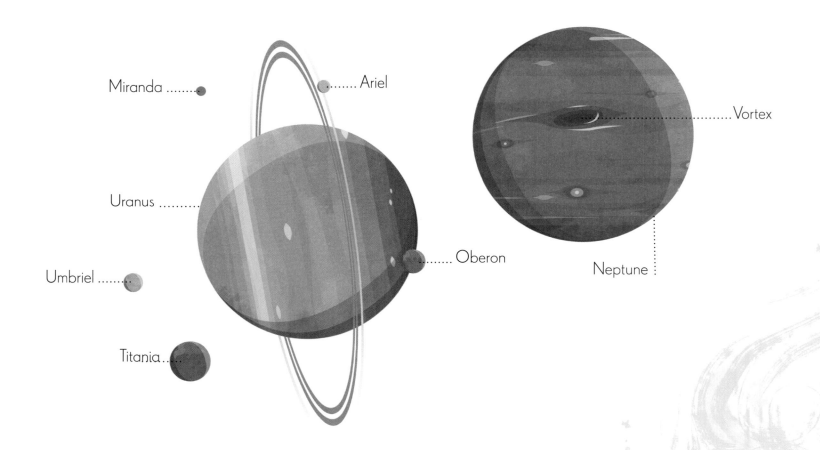

Miranda ........

........ Ariel

Uranus ..........

........ Oberon

Umbriel ........

Titania ..........

Vortex

Neptune

# Pluto

For a long time Pluto was thought to be the ninth and smallest planet. But new discoveries revealed similar objects living in our distant Solar System. Pluto was put in a new category and we now call it a dwarf planet.

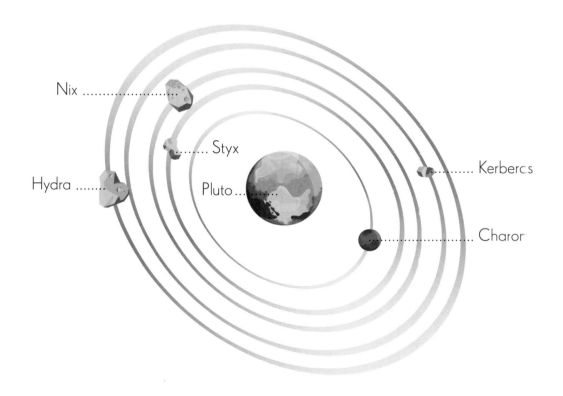

Nix

Styx

Hydra

Pluto

Kerberos

Charon

# The Milky Way

Scientists think that our home galaxy, the Milky Way, contains around 200-400 billion stars. NASA telescopes use infrared and X-ray light to reveal the beauty of the Milky Way, seen on the reverse of this poster.

# Stars

Stars can live for billions of years. It takes a long time for their light to reach us since they're so far away-so looking up at night means gazing into the past. The stars on the other side of this poster were photographed by the Hubble Space Telescope.

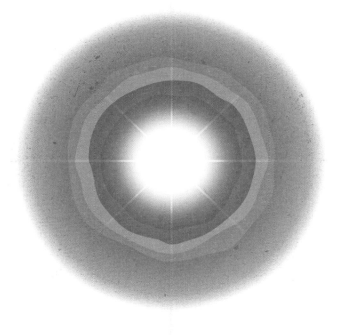

# Star clusters

Groups of stars are called clusters. Our sun probably formed within a cluster that has now spread across the galaxy. The stars in the cluster Pleiades, shown on the other side of this poster, are thought to be around 130 million years old!

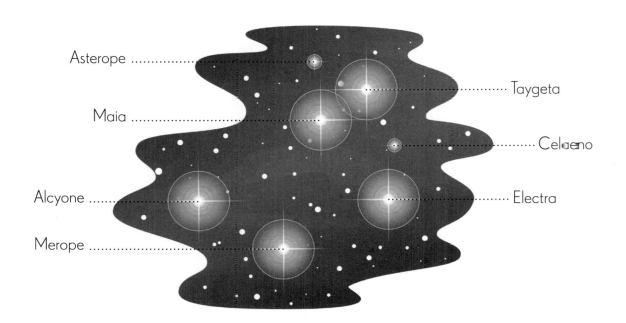

Asterope ·············

Maia ···············

Alcyone ···········

Merope ···········

··········· Taygeta

··········· Celaeno

··········· Electra

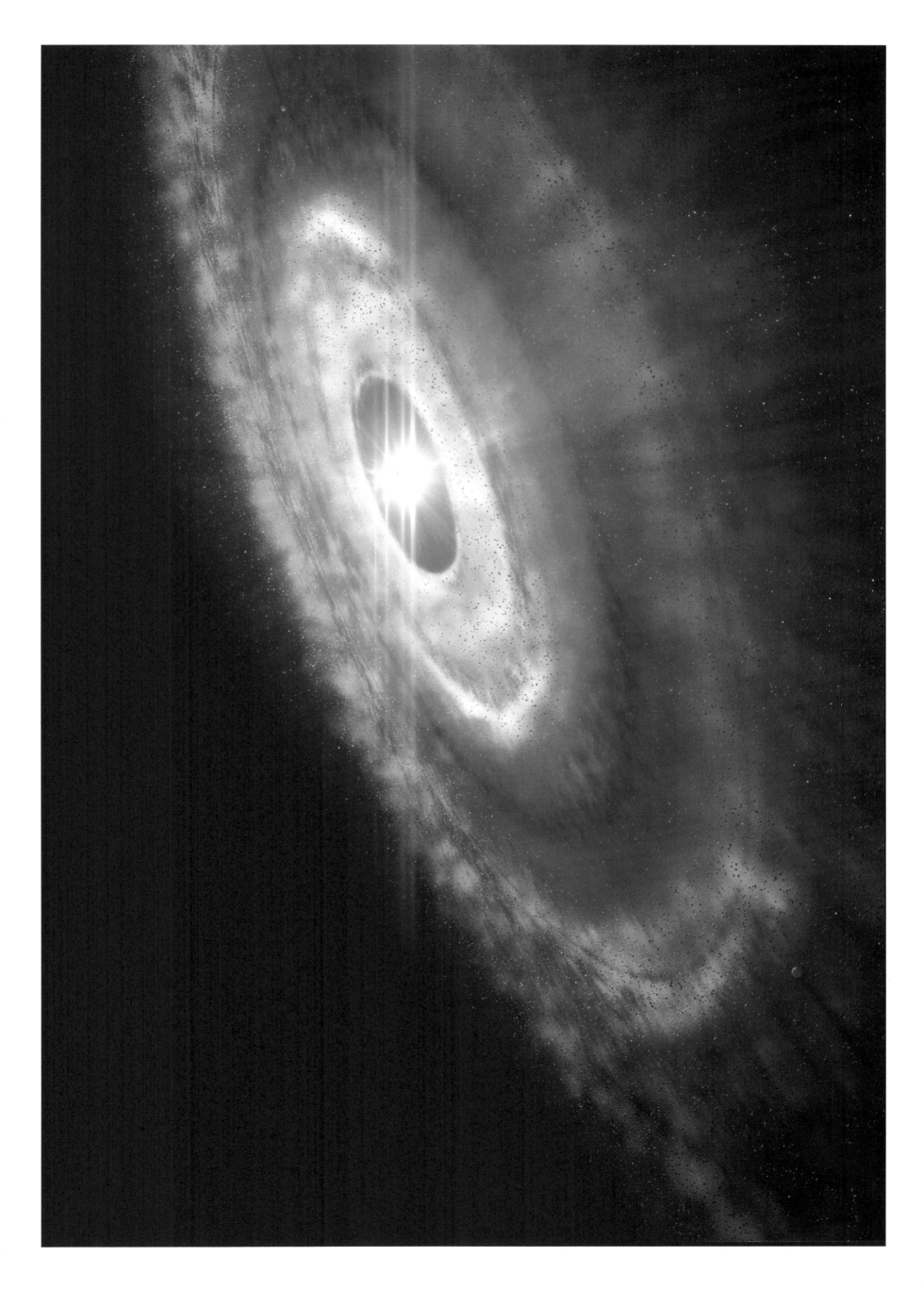

# Birth of a planet

Astronomers think that planets start out as protoplanetary disks that surround young stars. Inside these disks are the raw ingredients from which worlds can be made.

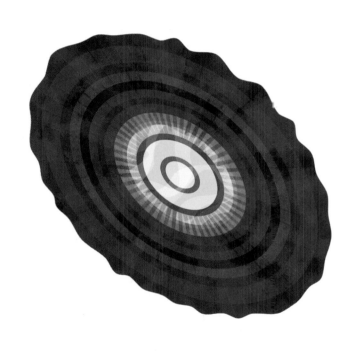

# Eta Carinae

Within the constellation Carina, there is a stellar system
called Eta Carinae. It is fascinating because one of its two
stars has recently experienced unimaginably huge eruptions.
Scientists think it is probably close to the end of its life.

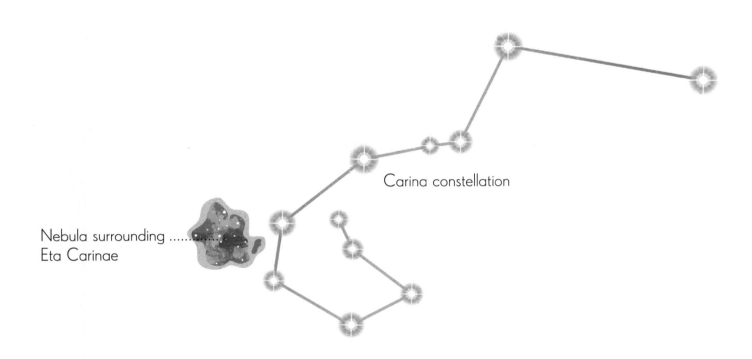

Carina constellation

Nebula surrounding ......
Eta Carinae

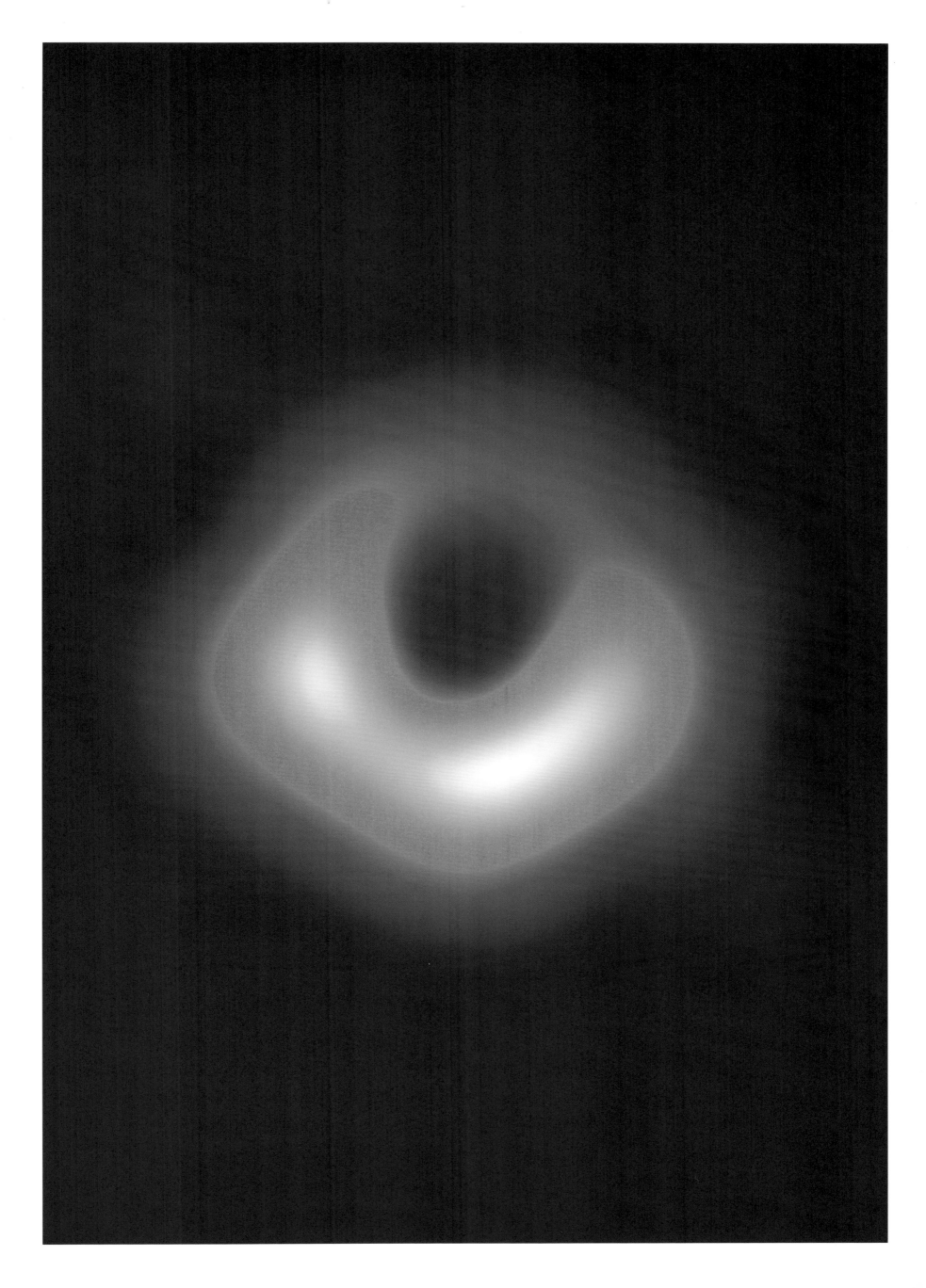

# Black hole

Black holes are among the most mysterious objects in the universe. Even the world's smartest scientists do not understand exactly how they work. The other side of this poster shows our best-ever view of a black hole's surroundings.

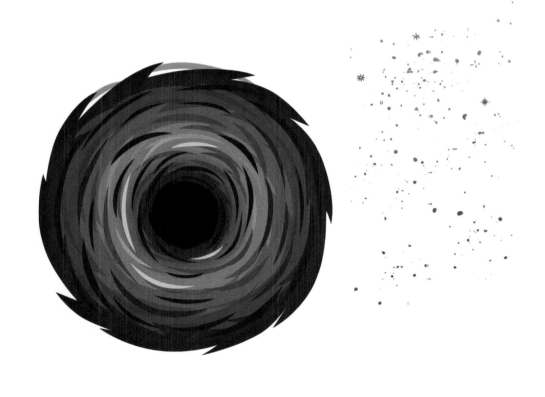

# Globular cluster

These extraordinary objects contain thousands of stars, all packed together in a ball. They could be the leftovers from smaller galaxies that were swallowed by our galaxy a long time ago.

.......... Globular cluster

# Dark nebula

These cosmic clouds of dust and gas can be found throughout outer space, lurking in the darkness. Pictured on the reverse of this poster is the Horsehead Nebula – it's easy to see how it got its name.

Dark nebula ........

# Reflection nebula

The image on the other side of this poster is Messier 78, from the Constellation Orion. The inner regions of this enormous reflection nebula appear to be shining an otherworldly blue color.

# Galactic Center

The infrared image on the other side of this poster reveals hundreds of thousands of stars in the hidden Galactic Center. The way stars move around it suggests there's a black hole lurking within.

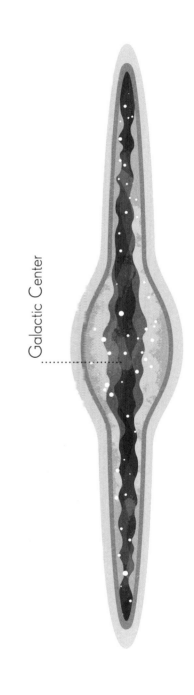

Galactic Center

# The Pillars
# of Creation

Found in the Eagle Nebula, about
5,870 light-years from Earth, these
billowing clouds of dust and gas give
us a glimpse into how stars form.

............ The Pillars
of Creation

# Supernova remnant

These clouds of rapidly expanding material surge out into the void where a star that has just died once lived. The image on the other side of this poster shows the visible part of a supernova remnant known as the Cygnus Loop.

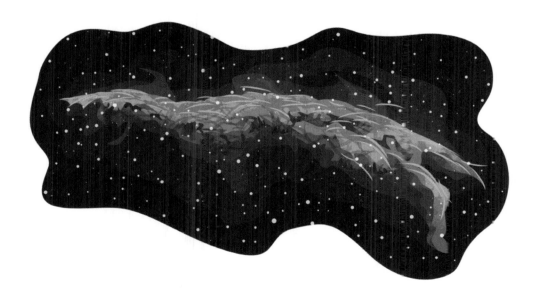

# The Andromeda Galaxy

This galaxy is racing in our direction at more than 244,000 miles (393,000 km) per hour! In around 6 billion years' time it will merge with the stars of our own Milky Way.

Spiral arm ......

# Spiral galaxy

Spiral galaxies usually have a central region of older, yellower stars and several curving "arms," where stars form and are flecked with glowing red nebulae. Pictured on the other side of this poster is Messier 74-comparable in size to our Milky Way.

# Lenticular galaxy

These galaxies are shaped a bit like the lenses found in magnifying glasses. The beautiful example on the reverse of this poster is known as the Spindle Galaxy, or NGC 5866. It is side-on to Earth, so we can see its shape perfectly.

Central bulge .......................................................

Lack of spiral arms

# Stephan's Quintet

These five faraway galaxies look close together, but the bluer-looking galaxy is much closer to us than the others. The illusion that it is so close to the others is created by the angle at which we're viewing them.

# Gravitational lens

This huge cluster of galaxies distorts space, as its immense gravity bends the path of light traveling toward us from galaxies behind it. This means our view of distant galaxies is magnified and smeared, making them look like thin arcs of light.

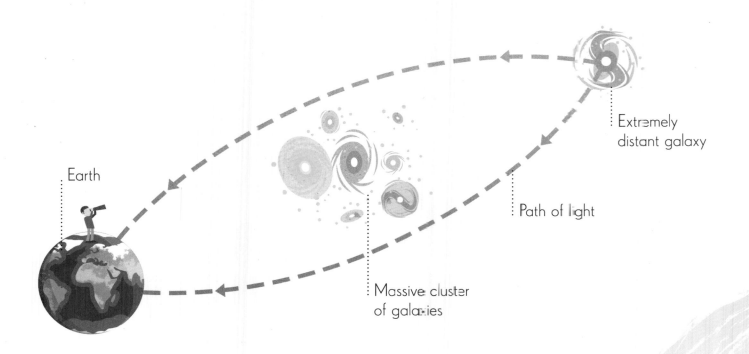

Earth

Extremely
distant galaxy

Path of light

Massive cluster
of galaxies